REAL
DAVVENING

Jewish Prayer as a
Spiritual Practice and a
Form of Meditation
for Beginning and
Experienced Davveners

Yitzhak Buxbaum

D1600480

Volume One
THE JEWISH SPIRIT BOOKLET SERIES

THE JEWISH SPIRIT BOOKLET SERIES

Yitzhak Buxbaum, Editor

THE JEWISH SPIRIT BOOKLET SERIES on Jewish spirituality will answer such questions as: "How can I be a Jew in a meaningful way?" and "How can I be a Jew so that it affects my life deeply?" The booklets will attempt to provide a gateway to a deeper and more fulfilling involvement in Judaism for both beginners and committed Jews by offering elevated ideals and practical help to those seeking to make real spiritual progress.

The booklet format has been chosen so that essential and exciting teachings on Jewish spirituality and mysticism can be made available in an accessible and affordable way to the largest audience. The goal is to further Jewish renewal by reuniting the Jewish people with the rich spiritual treasures of Judaism.

Topics in Jewish spirituality will be treated in a way to interest people Jewishly learned and those well advanced on the spiritual path, but also to interest and be fully accessible to Jews who are non-scholars and to those just beginning their Jewish quest.

JEWISH SPIRIT booklets will try to make Jewish spirituality truly popular. They will be be inspiring, concise, informative, and useful. They will be authored by people of different religious tendencies, who represent a broad spectrum of those working to renew Jewish spirituality.

Titles in THE JEWISH SPIRIT BOOKLET SERIES:

> Vol. 1 Real Davvening
> Vol. 2 An Open Heart

Some forthcoming titles:

> How to Develop Faith and Trust in God
> The Essentials of Jewish Meditation
> Jewish Mysticism in a Nutshell
> An Introduction to Traditional Jewish Mantras

We welcome submissions for inclusion in the series. Please send manuscripts or proposals to THE JEWISH SPIRIT BOOKLET SERIES (see address on p. 48).

ISBN 0-9657112-1-8

CONTENTS

A NOTE TO THE READER

This booklet is intended to be used by both women and men. Although the language in the booklet refers to God as King, Father, He, and Him, God is not corporeal, has no gender, and is not a male. Men and women are made in God's image (Genesis 1:27), and God has both masculine and feminine traits.

Dedication

Hannah the prophetess, say the rabbis, was the first to call God: the Lord of Hosts. And they say that she was one of the Lord's host on earth. There are angels—divine messengers and servants—Above and angels Below. There are also "female" as well as "male" angels (*Yalkut Chadash,* Mal'achim, 63 and 93).

Hannah was a woman of prayer and the rabbis derived some of the ways of prayer from what the Torah tells about her. They also say that Hannah went to the Temple frequently to prostrate before God and that was why her prayers were heard and answered.

This booklet is dedicated to three dear friends, who, like Hannah the prophetess, are women of prayer and angels of the Lord of hosts—Yicara Weisskoff, Mina Korman, and Dina Jacobs. May their light shine ever more strongly to their loved ones and to all Israel.

This booklet is also dedicated to my beloved mother, Jeanette Buxbaum, of blessed memory, who hardly knew how to pray, but who was an angel in my life.

INTRODUCTION
DAVVENING
(THE JEWISH WAY OF PRAYER)

Most teaching on Jewish prayer seeks to familiarize people with the structure of the prayer service or to explain the meaning of the various prayers or the theology of prayer, why we pray and so on. This booklet has another purpose—to teach you how to pray so that prayer works as a spiritual practice, so that it moves you spiritually. The goal is for you to achieve during prayer an elevated state of mind so that you actually taste and experience the nearness of God. That is what I mean by "real davvening."

Hasidic literature particularly contains many techniques to achieve this kind of davvening. Most of these techniques are fairly simple, such as controlling one's glance in order to concentrate better. These hasidic davvening practices are the basis of this booklet. If you follow them your praying will be immeasurably higher than before. You will get deep satisfaction from davvening and will experience the profound pleasure and joy of the nearness of God.

Many people today find prayer difficult. Somehow prayer doesn't seem to provide enough reward or satisfaction for them to see it as their pathway to spiritual fulfillment. But this lack of enthusiasm for prayer is primarily due to the fact that most people have not been taught how to pray. The rote praying that many people are accustomed to and that fails to provide powerful results is not the same as real davvening.

Prayer is a form of meditation and to benefit from any meditation you have to learn and apply the proper methods. Only by knowing *how* to pray can you really davven and progress spiritually by davvening. Sometimes this takes time; you can't expect to reach the final goal in your first attempts. Because you find no pearls the first time you dive in the ocean you must not conclude that there are no pearls there. You must dive again and again to find them. You can find God by prayer, but you must persevere. If you try even a few practices from this booklet, you will be encouraged to persist in your effort when you experience the life and vitality they infuse into your davvening.

Both beginning and experienced davveners, men and women can benefit by using the many traditional meditation techniques for prayer. Once people realize that there is something to learn about davvening as a spiritual practice, we will be on the path to a renewal of Jewish prayer. The following parable, used by hasidim of an earlier generation to explain their attempt to revive prayer, helps to clarify our situation today.

There was once a king who so loved music that he directed his musicians to play before him each morning. The musicians came to the palace and performed, to obey the king's command, but also because they loved and respected the king and valued their chance to be in his presence. So every morning they played for the king with enthusiasm and delight. For many years all went well. The musicians enjoyed playing each morning for the king and the king enjoyed listening to their music.

When, at last, the musicians died, their sons sought to take their places. But, alas, they had neither mastered the art of their fathers nor had they kept their instruments in proper condition. Worse still, the sons no longer loved the king as did their fathers. They just blindly followed their fathers' custom of arriving each morning at the palace to perform. But the harsh sounds of their music were so offensive to the king's ear that after a time he ceased listening.

But then some of the sons developed a renewed love and reverence for the king, however pale compared to the love and reverence of their fathers, and they realized that the king had stopped listening to their uninspired music. Although they wanted to perform to honor the king, they recognized that their inadequate skills made them unworthy to play before him.

So they set about the difficult task of relearning the forgotten art that should have been their inheritance from their fathers. Every day, before coming to the king, they spent time tuning their instruments. Upon entering the palace concert room and hearing the racket of the other musicians, they sought out an obscure corner for themselves where they could play undisturbed. They also remained long after the other musicians had departed, so that they might improve their skill. And in their homes they continued to practice and to struggle with their instruments as best they could.

The king was aware of their efforts and was pleased, for even though they did not play with the same talent as their fathers, still they strove, to the best of their abilities, to once more bring pleasure and joy to the king. Thus was their music received by the king with favor.[1]

One lesson of this parable is that if we want to progress spiritually by davvening, we must develop our davvening skills. But an even more important lesson is that we must davven with devotion, for only devotion wins God's favor.

REAL DAVVENING TO REACH GOD

There are many goals in praying, but the primary one is to draw close to God. His nearness and intimacy should be felt and experienced. Our relationship to God must not remain a mere concept, but must be fulfilled in reality. Judaism's fundamental teaching about prayer is that a person can communicate and speak with God and feel His answering presence.

Let us begin then to consider how you can achieve real davvening. First and foremost, you must understand that davvening is a form of meditation. One of the main times we focus and concentrate our attention most fully in daily life is when speaking to another person. Therefore, speech can be a way to meditatively focus attention on the Divine Person.

Because davvening is a form of meditation, focus and concentration are essential to its practice. One aspect of that concentration involves removing external and internal distractions that prevent you from directing yourself to God. One of the advantages of praying in a synagogue is that it is a holy building set aside for worship and, ideally, isolated from worldly influences. As you remove distractions and—this is the other main aspect of davvening—concentrate more and more on God, you will gradually begin to feel His presence. Most of the prayer techniques that we will discuss are simply ways to concentrate and focus more and more on the davvening and on God, until you alter your state of mind, enter the spiritual world, and actually experience God's nearness.

It is said that Rabbi Israel Baal Shem Tov, the founder of Hasidism, attained his exalted spiritual level because he prayed with fiery intensity.[2] A parable, which he sometimes told to his followers to instruct them specifically about

prayer,[3] contains the essence of his teachings about the
mystic quest for God and God-consciousness (*d'vekut*).
A king, by magic, surrounded his palace with many walls.
Then he hid himself within the palace. The formidable walls
were arranged in concentric circles, one inside the other, and
they grew increasingly larger as one approached the center.
They had fortified battlements and were manned by fierce
soldiers who guarded from above; wild animals—lions and
bears—ran loose below. All this was so that those who
approached would have proper awe and fear of the king and
so that not all who desired to approach would be allowed to
do as they pleased.

The king then had proclamations sent throughout the
kingdom saying that whoever came to see him in his palace
would be richly rewarded; he would be given a rank second
to none in the king's service. Who would not desire this? But
when many came and saw the outer wall's awesome size and
the terrifying soldiers and animals, most were afraid and
turned back. There were some, however, who succeeded in
scaling that wall and fighting past the soldiers and animals,
but then the second wall loomed before their eyes, even more
imposing than the first, and its guards even more terrible.
Seeing that, many others turned back.

Moreover, the king had appointed servants to stand behind
the walls to give money and precious stones to whomever got
beyond each wall. Those who had crossed one or a few walls
soon found themselves very rich and satisfied with what they
had gained from their efforts; so they too turned back. For
one reason or another, either from fear at the increasing
obstacles or satisfaction with the accumulated rewards, none
reached the king . . .

Except for the king's son. He had only one desire: to see the
face of his beloved father. When he came and saw the walls,
soldiers, and wild animals, he was astonished. He could not
understand how his dear father could hide himself behind all
these terrifying barriers and obstacles. "How can I ever reach
him?" he thought. Then he began to weep, and cried out,
"Father, Father, have compassion on me; don't keep me away

from you!" His longing was so intense that he had no interest in any rewards; indeed, he was willing to risk his life to attain his goal. By the courage of his broken heart, which burned to see his father, he ran forward with reckless abandon and self-sacrifice; he scaled one wall and then another, fought past soldiers and wild animals. After crossing the walls, he was offered money and jewels, but he threw them down in disgust. His only desire was to see his father. Again and again he called out to him.

His father the king, hearing his son's pathetic cries and seeing his total self-sacrifice, suddenly, instantaneously, removed the walls and other obstacles. In a moment they vanished as if they had never existed. Then his son saw that there were no walls, soldiers, or animals. His father the king was right before him, sitting on his majestic throne while multitudes of servants stood near to serve him and choirs sang his praises. Gardens and orchards surrounded the palace on all sides. And the whole earth shone from the king's glory. Everything was tranquil, and there was nothing bad or terrible at all.

Then the son realized that the walls and obstacles were a magical illusion, and that his father the king had never really been hidden or concealed, but was with him all the time. It was all just a test to see who truly loved the king.[4]

The simple meaning of this profound parable is that we are always in God's presence. The "walls" and obstacles that seem to separate us from Him are illusory. If we don't see Him, if we don't have the divine vision of the Godliness of all reality, it is because of our own spiritual deficiencies. But if we yearningly seek our Father in Heaven, we will find Him.

It is not accidental that the one to succeed in reaching the king is his son. We must realize that we are children of God, His sons and daughters, and that God is ever with us and does not intend to keep us separate from Him. The son in the parable succeeds because his love overcomes his fear. So must we increase our yearning and love for God until all barriers fall before us. In the parable, the son's forlorn cries of "Father, Father!" represent prayer. His readiness to die in his quest teaches the need for self-sacrifice (*mesirat nefesh*) for spiritual advance—and specifically for prayer. This parable undoubtedly depicts the Baal Shem Tov's own mystic quest, his fervent praying, and his moment of revelation. When praying, you must yearn, even desperately, to reach God. You must be determined to go forward and not be deterred, either by obstacles and distractions or by secondary pleasures, even the satisfactions of davvening. Like the son in the parable, you must be single-minded in prayer, to go forward, to go deeper and deeper, overcoming all barriers until you reach your goal—God's presence. The promise of the parable is that if you pray sincerely, from the heart, with self-sacrifice, God will reveal Himself to you.

All the teachings about davvening in this booklet have only one purpose: to help you to meditate deeply in prayer until you arouse your devotion and ignite your fervor for God. Remember that you will get back what you put in: The davvening techniques only work if used. The more of them you actually put into practice and perform, the better and more fulfilling your davvening will be.

Your attitude to davvening should be like that of a craftsman, who is interested not in theory but in getting the job done. The "job" during davvening is to somehow get close to God.

The practices will be discussed in the context of praying in a synagogue, but most of them apply also when praying at home or elsewhere.

You needn't understand Hebrew to really davven. But the davvening experiences of people who fully comprehend Hebrew and those who understand it only partially or not at all are somewhat different. We cannot, however, consider these differences in Hebrew knowledge every time they affect a practice discussed in this booklet. Neither can we take into account the different customs and styles of davvening in various synagogues.

Before the Service

◀ Entering the Synagogue

Rule one of davvening is to separate yourself from worldly thoughts, because your mind is typically jumping from one worry or plan to another, concerning your job, family, and so on. How can you begin to remove this kind of potential distraction to prayer? First, as you approach the synagogue, pause briefly before entering, to arouse your awe and love for God. Reflect that you are entering God's House and resolve to abandon your worldly preoccupations for the time you are inside.

A hasidic rabbi compared the entrance to a synagogue to a border between two countries, where you must have your luggage checked and any contraband must be thrown away before crossing. As you enter the synagogue or briefly pause at the doorway, whisper or pray mentally a short prayer, such as: "God, let me feel awe and love for You within the synagogue. Let me pray earnestly once inside and feel Your presence." Explicitly expressing your intention at the outset helps you to fulfill it.

◀ Choosing a Seat and Avoiding Talkers

Next is choosing a seat. It is best to sit fairly close to where the prayer-leader will be standing, so that you can hear well, participate fully, and feel involved in the service. Everyone knows the great difference distance makes in these matters. Sit in the same location each time you are in the synagogue, for then that place will turn your mind by habit to thoughts of prayer and to God.

Try to select a seat away from people you know to be "talkers." Avoid casual conversation in the synagogue sanctuary, particularly during the service, because it destroys any attempt at concentration. One cannot meditate and shmooze at the same time; one cannot go from a casual conversation with a friend to a profound conversation with God. Would a person meditating in a yoga center begin a conversation with the person meditating next to him? It makes as little sense for a person davvening in a synagogue to converse with his neighbor. Also, when you pray, you are sanctifying and dedicating your speech to God for a period of time; idly conversing during or immediately before or after prayer detracts from that purpose.

The noise of talkers will distract and irritate you and they may try to involve you in their conversations. So if someone who is a talker sits near you, simply move, but discreetly, so as not to offend. If someone tries to involve you in a conversation, be friendly in demeanor, but say politely, "I don't like to talk in the synagogue," or "during services." If people are disturbing you by their conversation during the services, quietly change your seat. Avoid asking them to be quiet, because some people who enjoy talking in synagogue may react to your request in an unpleasant way that will spoil your mood and ruin your attempt to accomplish something spiritually. In fact, for that same reason it is best to avoid a judgmental attitude about such people even within your own mind. Simply move and let it go at that.

◄ Preparing to Pray

After selecting your seat, if it is the morning service, and you wear a tallit and tefillin, put them on, while standing. As you put on the tallit, it is traditional to wrap it fully around your head, "tent-like," covering your eyes too, before putting it down to rest on your shoulders. While the tallit is over your head this way, you can briefly meditate on being intimately with God. Then sit down and, with eyes closed, calm yourself and put yourself in a peaceful mood.

Preparation for prayer is a key to real davvening. The Kotzker Rebbe said that the time spent in sharpening the axe is as important as the time spent in chopping down the tree. Since the essence of prayer is coming close to God, that should be the first thing you concentrate on. To scale a high wall, you first throw a grappling line over the top of the wall until its hook catches and, with that support, begin to climb up. So, first, you should attach yourself to God by a preparatory meditation, then you can begin to scale your way up—to higher spiritual states—by prayer.

How do you meditate to prepare for prayer? Such a meditation can have a number of elements, but the primary one is to simply focus on God. With eyes closed (or open, if you prefer), direct your attention to God. You can imagine the room as full of God's light, the aura of His glorious presence, which totally surrounds you—above, below, left, right, in front and back. You can also imagine God as before you and that you are looking at Him and He at you, face to face (see p. 34).

It is good to pray, asking for God's help in prayer, for example, "God, help me to pray as I should, in a way that will bring me close to You." You can also utter under your breath other spontaneous prayers that fit the moment, such as "God, let me feel Your presence in the synagogue. Let me pray to you without distraction and go deeper and deeper until I am in Your presence," and so on.

The whole prayer service will be elevated by what you attain in preparation. Such preparations can be brief or lengthy and can take one, three, five minutes or more, depending on your level in davvening. Of course, the amount of time you can devote to preparation depends on your arriving sufficiently early for services. But, aside from exceptional circumstances (such as arriving at the synagogue right before the prayers begin), you should try to engage in at least a minimal preparation—such as the one described in the preceding paragraphs. Begin with a preparation of a minute or so and then, as you feel more comfortable with the practice, increase from there.

Elements of a fuller preparation are in an appendix at the end of this booklet. This is not because they are unimportant—quite the opposite—but to avoid excessively concentrating at the beginning of our discussion on preparation for davvening and on more advanced stages of davvening.

If you have finished your preparation and are waiting for the service to begin, don't sit idly: Pick up a *Chumash* (Five Books of Moses), *siddur* (prayer-book), or other holy book and engage in some study. (In the *siddur* you can find and study the rabbinic text *Pirke Avot*, "The Ethics of the Fathers.") Torah study is also a preparation for prayer, especially if you study in a devotional way, remembering that the teaching is from The One Who Spoke and the World Came into Being. It is good to whisper a holy intention at the beginning of such study: "God, I'm studying this Torah to purify my mind and heart for prayer." The point is to not let your mind wander. You want to immerse it in holiness by constant holy activity and to go deeper and deeper into a meditative mood. Instead of studying Torah while waiting for the service to begin, you can also sit with closed eyes and meditate by repeating a holy name or phrase (see further on) or quietly whisper (or mentally offer) various personal prayers.

◄ Being with Others

Davvening in a synagogue represents a balance between being with people, to join with them in worship and to derive power from that togetherness, and being apart from people in your own meditative world with God. But, certainly, being friendly is an essential part of Judaism. Traditionally, a person is supposed to utter, before praying, his or her resolve to fulfill the commandment, "you shall love your neighbor as yourself." This is a part of a preparation for praying, because opening your heart to your fellow humans helps you open your heart to God. So, if you have time during your moments of preparation, say: "God, I resolve to love my fellow Jews and all people. Let me join now with the Jews davvening here with me." When uttering this sentence, you can also look around at the other congregants and think that all those present, like you, have come to worship God, that they are in God's image and are His children, and that by loving them you can express your love for Him. Have compassion on them, even with their faults, and reflect that they too, in their hearts, yearn to serve God.

Greeting other congregants warmly before the services begin is a good preparation for opening yourself to greet the Divine Presence in prayer. Try to do this without encouraging a conversation. You can intend, as you greet people, to fulfill the commandment to love your neighbor.

Although the counsel against conversation during services (and immediately before and after) should not be considered as totally without exceptions, exceptions should be rare, for the more you converse, the less you will benefit spiritually from the services.

The Service

◄ Continuity and Depth

It is a principle of all Jewish spiritual practice to avoid any interruptions in a religious activity. As applied to prayer and the synagogue service, this means that you should strive to constantly and uninterruptedly meditate, whether by praying, singing, listening to the prayer-leader, meditating silently, or devotedly watching a Torah scroll being taken out of the Ark. The goal is to build up spiritual power. When you interrupt your davvening you destroy what you are working to accomplish. It is like trying to fill a pail with water—and at the same time punching holes in the bottom. *That* is the reason to avoid idle conversation and other distractions during prayer; it is not just a matter of "being strict." (If you are a parent who must care for children during the service, see p. 34.)

Therefore, to continuously meditate while davvening, you should participate in every part of the service and every communal prayer without exception, not neglecting parts that others may slight. If other people are inattentive during the *Kaddishes* or *Mi sheberachs,* or begin to talk during the Torah reading, that is their loss; don't make their mistake. To participate most fully, learn all the customs of the service and all the communal responses. Recite every *baruch hu uvaruch sh'mo!* ("Blessed is He and blessed is His name") and *amen!* with *kavvanah* (focused attention) and energy. (See the Glossary for unfamiliar Hebrew words and phrases in this and following paragraphs.)

Although you should try to participate in every part of the service you can make exceptions, in order to increase your *kavvanah,* by skipping certain parts in order to engage in another spiritual activity at that time. See further on.

Kaddishes are placed between sections of the prayer service and have a special potency to elevate you to a higher spiritual level, if you recite the responses of *amen* and *y'hei sh'mei rabba* ("May God's great name be blessed") etc. loudly, with all your concentration and energy. (Each *Kaddish* has a number of *amens* and one *y'hei sh'mei rabba*. Learn when and how to respond, if you don't know, by paying attention when others respond.) Once you know the responses, you will be able to listen with full concentration to the prayer-leader (or to mourners reciting the Mourner's *Kaddish*), with closed eyes, and vigorously utter the responses. Try reciting *Kaddishes* with *kavvanah* and you will see the powerful effect it has.

The essence of davvening is continuous concentration on God and Godliness throughout the prayer service.

A parable explains that if a person sleeps fitfully, half asleep, half awake, waking and sleeping on and off, she cannot reach the peaceful state of deep sleep that powerfully refreshes the mind. Only by continuous, uninterrupted sleep can she sink into a profound, refreshing slumber. Similarly, if a person prays fitfully, on and off, concentrating for awhile and then turning her attention elsewhere, she cannot reach the state of profound God-consciousness that transforms and refreshes her mind by its peace and joy.[5]

By continuous concentration during the service, you will be able to descend into a deeper and deeper meditative mood.

A parable tells of a woodsman who chopped trees and sold the lumber to make a living, who once went into the forest and encountered a sage studying there in seclusion. The sage greeted him and said, "Go forward." The woodsman followed the sage's advice and found a stand of trees of superior wood that made excellent lumber. Gratified, he took out his axe and was about to set to work. But then he thought, "The sage told me to go forward, not to stop when I found some good trees." So he went forward, still deeper into the forest and found a stand of rare trees of the most valuable lumber. He was about to celebrate his good fortune when he realized that the sage had told him, "Go forward." Again he went further and deeper into the forest, until he found a silver mine. He went further and found a gold mine, still further, and found a diamond mine.

If you go deeper and deeper in prayer your spiritual rewards will increase more and more, until finally you will be in the presence of God.

✺ Your Glance

How can you focus during prayer to go deeper?

One prime way to retain concentration is to control your glance. When meditating, you don't look around this way and that. So don't look around the synagogue aimlessly, at the people or elsewhere. Keep your eyes on the *siddur,* or on the Ark (which contains the Torah scrolls and therefore has a great manifestation of Godliness), or on the walls, floor, or ceiling, or out the window at the sky (whose unitary expanse reminds one of heaven and inspires religious feeling). If you wear a tallit, you can cover your head with it, which removes your peripheral vision and concentrates your eyes on the *siddur.* The rabbis say that viewing the letters of the prayers in the *siddur* helps concentration and arouses enthusiasm. But it is also helpful to keep your eyes closed occasionally during the service, which you are able to do more often if you have memorized some of the prayers. The point is to generally avoid looking at the other congregants (including the prayer-leader). Why? Because there are no more powerful distractions to prayer than viewing a human face or overhearing a conversation.

Although other people actually manifest a great light of Godliness, because they are created in the divine image, we are usually not receptive to that aspect of their being. However, when one rises, during prayer, to a spiritual level where one becomes calm and established in a meditative mood and grounded in an awareness of God's presence, then one *can* look in the faces of other congregants and, instead of losing one's concentration, be inspired further. But this is also a matter of experience. If you see that, even before reaching that higher spiritual level, looking at others inspires you, do so.

A particular problem in davvening arises from the fact that the ordained prayers are recited from a book, the *siddur*, and most of the time we are looking in the *siddur*. Do not, however, confuse davvening with reading. Be sure you davven *to* God.

◄ Utter the Words

You must utter the words of the service, moving your lips. Reading the prayers silently is not davvening. (Personal prayers, on the other hand, whether offered during the service or at other times, can be uttered either mentally or verbally.) You should recite all the communal responses, such as those in the *Kaddish*, loudly, but whisper the main prayer of the service, the *Amidah* (the Standing Prayer), although in a way that you can hear yourself. There are a number of profound spiritual reasons why prayers must be uttered aloud, most simply because "voice arouses *kavvanah*," but also because the effort needed to audibly utter the words expresses and furthers your commitment to really davven.

◄ Mean What You Say and Use Your Imagination

The most basic aspect of *kavvanah* is to mean and intend the words of the prayers as you say them, and to say them with faith. If you feel yourself losing touch with God or that your faith is "slipping" during the service, you can passionately whisper, "God, I believe in You!" Verbally affirming your faith is actually a prayer for faith. A powerful thought, which you can occasionally remind yourself of during the service, is to believe that God is listening to you as you speak. You may pray in the merest whisper, yet God hears every word. God, who hears the footfall of an ant, certainly listens to your words.

Be in tune with the words you are reciting: When a verse is about joy, be joyful, when it focuses on God's greatness, feel awe, etc. Since we should always be joyful when davvening, use the many verses that refer to joy to arouse such feelings.

Visualization can powerfully aid davvening. Try frequently, in verses where it is relevant, to briefly and momentarily visualize what you are saying.

For example, when you are reciting Psalm 148 in the morning service, when you say "Praise the Lord . . . Praise Him . . . sun and moon . . . [and] stars"—Visualize the sun in the sky, or the moon and stars at night. Imagine yourself calling to them to praise God. "Let every creature praise the Lord . . . fruitbearing trees and cedars, beasts, cattle, creeping things and birds, kings of the earth and all the nations, princes and rulers of the earth, young men and maidens, elders and children, let them all praise the Lord . . ." Visualize all the trees and plants on the globe silently praising God and all the animals vocally praising Him by their many calls and sounds. Picture in your mind all the many nations of the earth. If you are near a window, you may be able to look out and see the sky and the sun (or moon and stars) or the trees when you mention them, perhaps you can also see some pigeons, sparrows, or other birds; look around you at young men and women, children and elders in the synagogue, and so on.

◀ In the Presence: The Sh'ma and the Amidah

The tradition requires that you make a special attempt during the Sh'ma (the Hear O Israel Prayer) and the Amidah, the two main prayers of the synagogue service, to imagine yourself in the divine presence. When you recite the Sh'ma, close your eyes for the first verse and imagine yourself surrounded by God in all directions—left, right, front, back, above, below; His presence is within also. God is one and there is nothing but God. When you step forward in the Amidah, imagine, somewhat differently from the Sh'ma, that you are entering the divine presence, that God is before you and you are facing Him.

◄ Memorize the Prayers

Memorizing prayers greatly helps concentration in davvening. By reciting memorized prayers (in Hebrew or English), you can focus not only on reciting the correct words but on their meaning. Having a prayer memorized also allows you to close your eyes, to remove visual distractions, and achieve a higher level of *kavvanah*. The best way to memorize prayers is to concentrate, during davvening, on one at a time: Start with one of the more important prayers, such as the *Sh'ma* or the *Amidah,* and, after days or weeks, when it is memorized, go on to another.

◄ Repeat a Holy Phrase

One practice that helps to achieve continuity in prayer, so as to build up spiritual power and enter more and more deeply into meditation, is to repeat a holy phrase or call out a name of God. Repeating a holy phrase or name during minor delays or breaks in the service—such as when someone is walking up to the *bima* (elevated platform) for an *aliyah* (to be honored by being called up to recite the blessings for a part of the Torah reading) or when the prayer-leader is waiting for people to finish the *Amidah*—greatly increases your ability to continuously meditate during davvening. You can repeat, in Hebrew or English, traditional usages, such as: "Father in Heaven," (*abba shebashamayim*); "Master of the World," (*ribono shel olam*); "I have placed God before me always," (*shivitti HaShem l'negdi tamid*); "Blessed is the One and Only One," (*baruch yachid umeyuchad*), "Blessed is God's glorious kingdom forever and ever" (*baruch shem kevod malchuto l'olam va'ed*) or any other appropriate phrase or name. Although this is a very simple and easy practice, anyone who employs it will see immediate and great gains in the level he or she reaches during davvening.

◄ Reconnect Again and Again

Although you should not interrupt the service for extraneous concerns, you can interrupt your recitation of prayers to meditate briefly, perhaps with closed eyes, to reconnect again and again and remind yourself of God's presence. You can simply close your eyes and direct your inner glance to God. Or you can sit and sway to enhance your concentration and imagine yourself in the presence of God, or repeat a holy phrase or name, or utter a prayer, such as "God, all this is only for You!"

◄ Dealing with a Speeding Congregation

Since, unfortunately, many congregations speed through the service, you can easily get caught up, with them, in a race of recitation, so that you allow yourself to be overcome by the flood of words and lose your meditative focus. Occasionally "resting" by meditation—even if that means skipping prayers the prayer-leader and congregation are praying—allows you to maintain your composed meditative mood. (Certain parts of the service have priority over other parts and must be said. Consult your rabbi for specifics.) The rabbis teach that whether a person prays little or much, the essence is that his or her heart be directed to God. This radical teaching must be taken seriously and applied. One word of davvening recited with sincerity and devotion is worth more than all the words of the service if they are chanted emptily and mechanically.

Rabbi Eleazar HaKatan writes: "Recite the whole prayer service in order, but, as the rabbis say: 'Whether you do more or less, it is all the same, as long as your heart is turned to God' (*Berachot* 5) and: 'A little prayer with your heart directed ... is better than much without it' (Tur)."6 The Kotzker Rebbe said: "If by shortening your prayers you have greater concentration and *kavvanah*, it is preferable to shorten them, for a little with *kavvanah* is better than much without."[7]

◄ Personal Prayer

The fixed prayers of the synagogue services were ordained to facilitate group worship and because most people were unable to improvise prayers when needed. But personal prayer is actually the essence of prayer and during each service you should try to speak some of your own words to God (one traditional time for this is at the end of the *Amidah*). However, the speed of many services makes this important practice difficult if not impossible. One way to deal with this problem is to realize that no one else can tell what you are saying when you have your *siddur* open and are whispering prayers. When you want to utter a private prayer, simply move your lips and talk to God under your breath in English. The congregation may be saying one prayer, but you can be saying something else.

It is very helpful to intersperse short personal prayers during your davvening, particularly when there is some short break in the service. For example, say: "God, please draw me close to You!" Or: "God, let me do *tshuvah* (repent)!" Or: "Let me love my fellow humans. Let me treat everyone with respect, never saying a hurtful word." Although you may occasionally miss saying an ordained prayer because of this, this practice falls under the category of it being better to say little with *kavvanah* than much without, for uttering these short prayers inspires *kavvanah*.

◄ Devotion and Fervor

Prayer must be not only with *kavvanah* but with devotion and fervor. Continuously meditating in prayer is not enough. You must direct your mind to God but, as the rabbis say, God wants the heart. God wants your love, your awe, your fire, your all.

A lens can focus the sun's rays to start a fire. Use the lens of your meditation and concentration on the davvening to set your heart on fire for God.

One aspect of davvening with devotion and fervor is to davven with all your physical energy by raising your voice or by swaying, when standing or sitting, as it says in the Psalm verse of the Shabbat prayer *Nishmat,* "All my bones shall say, 'O Lord, who is unto like You?'" During the service, (if your synagogue's etiquette permits) you should occasionally stand, even if others remain seated, to wake yourself up and awaken your emotions. When you begin davvening you may feel dull, but by raising your voice and vigorously moving your limbs, you will arouse your feelings and inspire fervor. Spontaneously chanting the prayers (which is easier once you have entered the spirit of the davvening), in Hebrew or English, also helps concentration. Chanting and swaying have similar functions. Both are rhythmical movements (of voice and body) that reflect the movement of the Spirit; they are inherently "spiritual."

◀ For God Alone

Don't allow shame before others to inhibit you during prayer. To davven devotedly you must learn to ignore how you appear to other people. If, as you davven, you are aware of other people and concerned about what they are thinking of you, how can you be aware of God? If you are self-conscious, how can you be God-conscious? Today, piety is often unappreciated and misunderstood, and it can be difficult, especially for shy people, to stand out by even the least signs of fervent davvening. But once others see that you are sincere, they will usually admire your desire to truly pray. Regardless, the rabbis say, "Better to be called a fool all your life than to be out of God's favor for a moment." Morever, there are ways to be fervent without being obvious (such as by "shouting in a whisper," i.e., exerting yourself, as if shouting, but emitting only a whisper; this technique allows you to express zeal without disturbing others or drawing attention to yourself).

You must also not demonstratively show off your piety. If you feel yourself becoming aware of other people, and suspect that you might be restraining yourself due to embarrassment or posing to impress others, utter a whispered declaration: "God, I intend my davvening only for You! Let me not be concerned with the other people present. If any contrary thoughts arise in my mind, I hereby nullify them completely, I don't want them at all."

◀ Gestures and Postures

When we speak with people, our body language of gestures and postures can express as much as our speech. The same is true when we speak with God.

Just as you would not usually cross your legs when talking to an important person, avoid sitting back comfortably, crossing your legs, and praying to God. As much as possible, keep an alert posture, to help focus your energies in davvening.

The tradition ordains certain movements during davvening, such as bowing, beating with one's fist on the breast, etc., at different points in the service. You should make these actions expressive and meaningful rather than automatic and empty. When you take three steps forward and back for the *Amidah*, which respectively represent entering and leaving the immediate presence of God, understand it that way. When you bow, bow in reverence and humility. And so on.

Try to actually perform the movements specifically mentioned in various prayers, even if you move ever so slightly. If the prayer or Psalm says "Come, let us bow down," bow your head slightly, and so on.

Use expressive hand gestures that fit the prayers. You can clasp your hands or stretch them out beseechingly. Even slight gestures, hardly noticeable by others, can be very meaningful. If when your hand is resting palm down on your thigh you merely turn it palm up in supplication, while you are praying or listening to the prayer-leader, it expresses a world of meaning. It is also very helpful to occasionally look up (to and "through" the ceiling), because, although God is everywhere, looking up has its own symbolic meaning that works on our consciousness.

◄ The Prayer-Leader

It is possible, in worldly matters, to allow someone else to speak for you, while you totally identify with his or her presentation of your thoughts or needs. In the same way, you can consider the prayer-leader to be chanting or speaking for you to God. You can, for instance, close your eyes and direct your inner gaze to God (perhaps leaving your hand, palm upward, on your thigh), and consider the prayer-leader to be expressing your prayers (always do this for the prayer-leader's repetition of the *Amidah*). This can be tremendously effective. In fact, when you listen this way to the prayer-leader, since you do not then have to exert your own effort to actually say the words or sing, you can devote all your concentration to the inner *kavvanah,* and enter more deeply into a meditative mood.

This same practice can also be extremely effective when the congregation is singing. Sometimes, instead of singing with them, make them your spokesman, while you concentrate on the *kavvanah* alone.

◄ The Torah Reading and the Sermon

When the Torah scroll is removed from the Ark and carried in procession around the synagogue, show your devotion and cultivate devotion by not waiting for it to reach you but by moving toward it. When kissing it, utter words such as: "God, may I do what is in Your Torah." When the Torah is being read, reflect that the Torah communicates God's Word. As you participate fully and follow the reading, try to find something that speaks to you and relates to your life and your service of God.

When listening to the sermon or Torah discourse, consider the rabbi or other teacher to be an agent of God, Who will send you teaching through that individual—regardless of the individual's personal qualities or the excellence of the sermon—if you listen receptively. You can whisper prayers before the Torah reading and before the sermon: "God, open my mind and heart to hear Your Word in the Torah reading" or "the sermon."

After the Service

After the service do not immediately begin a conversation or rush to leave. If possible, sit for a brief meditation, even if for only half a minute. Bind yourself to God so that what you have achieved spiritually during prayer does not quickly dissipate afterward. You can close your eyes and meditate by simply directing your inner gaze to God—imagine yourself looking at God and He at you. Or you can consider how to apply the inspiration you achieved during prayer to the rest of the day. If you cannot stay seated to meditate, meditate as you exit the sanctuary. And when you leave the synagogue, pause briefly at the doorway, just as you did when you entered, to reflect on what thoughts you are taking to your next activity, and try, as best you can, to take with you your renewed awareness of the presence of God.

A Promise

The hasidic rebbes often placed at the head of a list of instructions for attaining piety (which included prayer techniques such as those in this booklet) the phrase from Leviticus: These are the things "which if a person does them, he shall *live* by them."[8] They said that if you performed these spiritual practices, they would make your Judaism come *alive*.

Note that the verse says "if a person *does* them." Merely reading about meditation or davvening will not help you spiritually. But by following even some of the prayer techniques in this booklet, you have the rebbes' promise that you will reach spiritual levels in your davvening that you never before attained. Your davvening will become deeper and more joyful and you will feel and experience the holiness, beauty, and sweetness of the Divine Presence.

The rebbes say that thrilling descriptions of spiritual goals, such as blissfully experiencing the Divine Presence, are like a tempting feast spread out on the table before your eyes. But you need a spoon to partake. The practices in this booklet can provide you with a spoon. May you seek God's nearness and may He draw you close.

The Lord is near to all who call upon Him, to all who call upon Him in truth.

QUESTIONS AND ANSWERS

Q: What should I do if I can't keep up with the *minyan*?

A: Usually this happens because the congregation is davvening too fast. Or because your Hebrew is not fluent enough; or, if it is, and you could keep up, because you want to pray slowly and not race. One solution to this problem is to simply skip parts of the service (as mentioned previously, consult your rabbi to learn which prayers have priority and which can be skipped if necessary). For example, while the *minyan* is saying two Psalms, you can say one. In fact, sad to say, many prayer-leaders, who may be under pressure from congregants to davven quickly, only pretend to recite the whole prayer or Psalm. They say just the beginning, let their eye race over the middle, and then they say the end. There is no way a person can say the whole prayer and keep up with a prayer-leader who does this.

The rabbis taught that whether a person prays little or much, the main thing is if his or her heart is directed to God. The radical nature of this teaching should be understood and applied in practice: If you can't keep up with the *minyan*, it's better to skip complete parts of the service and say the remaining parts completely, than to pretend to say everything, while actually skipping over the middle or cutting off the end of many sections. Even if you *can* keep up with the *minyan,* by davvening quickly like everybody else, it's still better to skip parts of the service, and say the rest with full concentration, than to say the whole thing in a confused state of mind while racing through one prayer after another, hardly knowing what you're saying.

You should also make a rule for yourself not to worry too much about where the *minyan* is. Generally, try to keep up with the *minyan,* except for times when you're digressing, when saying a personal prayer on your own, and so on; but otherwise, don't worry about it. Don't allow concern with where the *minyan* is to disrupt the meditative mood you're trying to establish. The worst that can happen is that you'll miss something or have to turn to someone nearby and ask him or her for the correct place in the *siddur.*

Q: What should I do if I can read Hebrew but only partially understand what I'm reading?

A: Increasing your knowledge of Hebrew will help your davvening tremendously, but the main thing is not to let your lack of Hebrew prevent you from having the spiritual experience of davvening. People often davven in Hebrew and continually look over to the English to see what it means. But if you find that glancing back and forth prevents you from attaining a meditative focus during the davvening, try reciting some or even many of the prayers in English; for example, reciting the communal prayers that are sung, in Hebrew, and reciting the prayers that are said individually, in English. But if you are reciting prayers in Hebrew, with little or only partial understanding, consider these words in the holy tongue as vehicles carrying your innermost thoughts and deepest spiritual longings to God. While uttering the Hebrew words, think thoughts related to the davvening and focus your mind on God. When the congregation sings a melody for a prayer, consider the spiritual message of the melody as primary and the words as secondary. Join in the singing and let the song carry your soul heavenward.

Q: When I don't know what's going on in the service or can't find the place in the prayerbook, I get confused . . .

A: Learn to accept that sort of embarrassment or confusion. Use such situations to develop some humility. You're not perfect. And you're closer to God when you're embarrassed and humble. You can also make it a habit to always ask someone nearby to help, to tell you the place in the *siddur* or what's happening. People are anxious to help you, and this kind of contact makes you feel you're friends with everybody there.

Q: How can I concentrate on the service in a meditative mood, and not interrupt, if I have to care for my daughter? Sometimes I have to talk to her or take her to the bathroom. She's also of an age where, every once in a while, I want to explain to her what's going on during the service, to teach her.

A: The way to prevent interaction with your child from interrupting your meditation is to look at her as being in the image of God. Meditate on *her* when you turn your attention to her. What does this mean? It means that one minute you're looking in the *siddur,* speaking to God, the next minute you're looking at your daughter, who is in God's image and is also God's daughter, speaking to her. To "meditate" on your child means that, when you turn your attention to her, you occasionally think thoughts such as these as you talk to her or care for her.

Q: You've spoken about directing your inner gaze to God and looking at God face-to-face. What do you mean?

A: We all know what it means to face and direct yourself to a presence, to another person, who is right before you. And we know what it feels like when someone is in front of you, looking at you face-to-face. I mean something like that. Just as intimate. God is not a human, but has a presence or "face," so to speak. Imagine the Divine Presence in front of you. God is looking at you, and you look back.

PRAYER PREPARATION

There are many possible elements in an extended preparation for prayer, but you don't have to use all of them or the same ones or the same order every time. Below, I have placed them in at least one reasonable order. It will be helpful to write down an outline of headings of elements of a prayer preparation on a blank page of your *siddur,* to have it ready to hand. You can select elements from it during your time of preparation or follow them as listed. It is, in fact, easy to include all of them.

◀ Elements of Prayer Preparation

1. Torah study—Before beginning to study from a holy book, state that your intention is to purify your mind for prayer. Study according to the time available and enough to prepare for prayer, but not so much that you forget about praying. Even a few minutes of devotional Torah study is beneficial.

2. Repentance—Reflect on your faults and resolve to change your ways.

3. *Tzedaka* (Charity)—Put some money into a charity box, if one is available at the synagogue; if one is not available, vow (verbally promise God) to donate after the service. Have a receptacle for this purpose at home; for when davvening there. As you put the money in, pray: "May I have love for all people, particularly for the poor and needy. In the merit of this *tzedaka,* may my heart open and may I feel Your presence

when I pray." On a Sabbath or holiday, you can vow to give, stating your intention and the sum that you will give after the day. "I vow to give such-and-such a sum for charity" (but don't forget to give later).

4. Separate from this world—Resolve to remove from your mind worldly concerns that will hinder you from focusing on prayer and on God. You can think or say: "God, I now separate myself from any thoughts about my family, my job, etc. (mentioning matters that may be bothering you or that may intrude on your consciousness); now is not the time for such thoughts and I don't want them at all."

5. Longing—Silently long to be able to pray with devotion and fervor, or express your longing verbally: "God, I so much desire to pray with devotion and fervor," or "I long to pray in the right way and draw close to You."

6. Pray for God's help to be able to pray properly. "God, help me, etc."

7. Join with the people of Israel and with the *tzaddikim* (saints)—Say: "God, I now join myself with all Jews praying throughout the world, and specifically the people here with me, and I join myself with the holy people of this generation and of all past generations."

8. Love of people and forgiveness—To love God you must love and be at peace with your fellow humans. You must forgive them their sins against you and resolve to seek their forgiveness for your sins against them. Resentment and anger at another person are barriers to approaching God. After reflecting briefly on your relations with others and considering specific cases, you can say: "God, I resolve to love my fellow humans. I forgive those who have harmed or insulted me (if relevant, have specific individuals in mind); and I will ask forgiveness from those whom I have harmed or insulted (have them in mind) as soon as possible."

9. Love and fear of God—Arouse your love and fear (awe, reverence) of God by reflecting on or verbally expressing

these attitudes, for example, "God, I want to express my love for You and my reverence for You. And if I lack either, I beg You to fill me with love and reverence." This element is mentioned in #12 further on and included in the meditation for God-awareness in Appendix 2.

10. Overcome obstacles and barriers—Resolve to overcome any obstacles, barriers, and distractions that occur during prayer and to move forward into God's presence.

11. Self-sacrifice—Think or say: "I resolve now to pray with self-sacrifice, with all my energy and concentration, to reach You at all costs."

12. Meditate on God's presence.

   a. Meditate on God's presence or "glory" (aura) as light surrounding you and filling the room. Then close your eyes and, thinking of God as before you, direct your inner gaze to Him with love. Meditate on God as your Father, or in any other way you find helpful.

   b. There is a meditation for God-awareness that is frequently found in hasidic sources. It contains a number of elements and is often used either to prepare for prayer or during prayer, to become aware of God's presence with love and awe. See Appendix 2 for the content of this meditation.

13. Nullify foreign thoughts—Say: "God, I want to think only of the prayers and only of You. I don't want any foreign (extraneous) thoughts whatsoever. And if any foreign thoughts enter my mind while I am davvening, let them be nullifed and void. I don't want them at all!" This declaration can be repeated, as needed, during the service.

14. Reflect on what you will do during prayer, and resolve, for example, that you will control your glance, raise your voice, etc.

Most of these elements can be meditated on silently (mentally) or verbally. You can, for example, use one element after the other, in sequence, in a verbal prayer-meditation spoken to God, where you: Declare that you resolve to repent and to separate from worldly concerns while davvening, express your love and reverence for Him, express your determination to love other people, and so on. Glancing at the headings in the list, improvise as you go along. Say, for example: "God, I fully resolve to repent now and to change my ways, since I so much long to get close to you. I know that yesterday I did such-and-such and I'm ashamed of myself. I'll not do that again. And I separate myself now from all worldly concerns, from my worries about making a living, from worries about my tasks and errands for today, about my meeting later in the day with so-and-so, from my plans for going out tonight. I'll think now of nothing but You and the davvening. Everything else can wait." And so on.

A meditation briefly using all the elements in this list, except for the Torah study and the meditation for God-awareness in Appendix 2, may, minimally, require a little more than five minutes (the meditation in Appendix 2 takes another five minutes). A prolonged meditation to prepare for davvening is easier to do when davvening at home than in a synagogue.

A MEDITATION FOR GOD-AWARENESS

This meditation has three basic parts.

I. It initially focuses on two attributes of God: His greatness and His goodness. It is perhaps easiest to at least begin the meditation with closed eyes.

1) First, you meditate on God's greatness as the creator of the universe, from the farthest reaches of the galaxies to the smallest subatomic particles, from the infinite to the infinitesimal. God created all that exists, both inanimate and animate: this world, with its mountains and valleys, its oceans and rivers; all living creatures, plants and animals, including humans; the senses and their objects, all shapes, colors, sounds, and so on. The divine work of creation was not finished long ago but continues constantly: At every moment, the world emanates from God's being. The only support for the existence of any thing is the divine will that it exist. Were the Creator to remove the divine will for a moment, that thing would instantly cease to exist. This meditation on God's greatness is intended to arouse fear (awe) of God. After meditating this way, you can say: "God, let me be filled with awe at Your greatness!"

2) Next, you meditate on God's goodness, in creating everything only for the good of His creatures and because of His love for them, most particularly because of His desire to share His eternal bliss and joy with humans. This meditation is to arouse love for God and it is deeper and more basic than

the first meditation, which is to arouse awe, because while that meditation is on the creation itself, this one is on its inner purpose. After meditating this way, you can say: "God, let me be filled with love for You because of Your goodness and love for us!"

II. The meditation must engage not only your mind but your emotions. To enhance the potential for these thoughts of God's greatness and goodness to elicit the emotions of awe and love, you continue by applying the concepts of the meditation to the present moment, to the here and now, and to yourself. You meditate that: "God is creating the whole universe and everything in my immediate environment now— (perhaps) the room I am in, (open your eyes) the shapes and colors I see (close your eyes), the sounds I hear, the floor beneath my feet, the chair on which I am sitting, the air I am breathing. God is creating me also, my body, my senses that allow me to experience this surrounding reality, my feelings, the thoughts I am now thinking, my consciousness, at this very moment. Why? Only because of God's goodness and love, and His desire to share His essential delight and joy with His creatures and with me. *God is here now with me this very moment.* I am surrounded and filled with divine light and love and joy.

III. Now, focus your inner gaze on God and imagine Him looking back at you. Just sit silently, basking in the radiance of His presence, meditating on God's love for you and on returning that love.

You can perform this meditation mentally or verbally, improvising according to the preceding sequence and directing your words to God. For example: "God, I know that You have created the whole universe, from the galaxies in the farthest reaches of space, to the smallest subatomic particles. I know that You have created everything that exists, both inanimate and animate . . . , etc. Let me be filled with awe of You." And so on.

◀ Outline of the Meditation:

I. 1) God's greatness—your awe
   2) His goodness and love—your love

II. Here and now, with me

III. Face-to-face, returning God's love

This meditation has a few basic parts. You can learn the outline and improvise the details.

For Further Reading

See Yitzhak Buxbaum's *Jewish Spiritual Practices* (Jason Aronson Inc., 757 pages), chapters 5 and 6, for many more davvening practices. If you would like to purchase that book, please see the information on p. 43.

Notes

1. This parable has been adapted from a parable used by Rabbi Levi Yitzhak of Berditchev to explain the hasidic attempt to revive prayer. See S. Dresner, *The World of a Hasidic Master*: Levi Yitzhak of Berditchev (New York: Shapolsky, 1986), p. 16, quoting *Vikucha Rabba*, p. 38.

2. *Keter Shem Tov*, p. 22b.

3. He sometimes told it before the shofar blowing on Yom Kippur.

4. In *Sefer Baal Shem Tov* (vol. 2, pp. 235f.) there are 8 versions of this parable. My version is a composite.

5. This parable from the Maggid of Mezritch is found in *Midrash Ribesh Tov*, II, p. 30a (59), quoting *Derech Hasidim*.

6. The *Shulchan Aruch of Rabbi Eleazar HaKatan*, laws of synagogue and prayer, #5, #6.

7. *Sneh Bo'er b'Kotzk*, p. 63.

8. Leviticus 18:5.

GLOSSARY

Aliyah — When an individual is honored by being called up to the *bima* (synagogue platform) to recite the blessings for part of the Torah reading.

Amidah — The Standing Prayer. The weekday *Amidah* is called the *Shemoneh Esreh,* the Eighteen-Blessing Prayer.

Baruch hu uvaruch sh'mo! — "Blessed is He and blessed is His name." A communal response recited immediately after the prayer-leader chants God's name at the beginning of a blessing.

Kaddish — A prayer expressing hope for the sanctification of God's name and the coming of His kingdom on earth. A number of kinds of *Kaddish* occur throughout the service, one of them being the Mourner's *Kaddish.*

Kavvanah — Focused attention.

Minyan — A prayer-quorum of ten.

Mi sheberach — A blessing recited from the synagogue platform on behalf of an individual.

Rebbe — A leader of a hasidic sect. A rebbe is always a rabbi but few rabbis are rebbes. Rebbes are often called after a town, for example, the Kotzker Rebbe from Kotzk.

Y'hei sh'mei rabba — "May God's great name be blessed," etc.

IF YOU ENJOYED THIS BOOKLET AND BENEFITTED FROM IT

☐ Why not send gift copies to friends or donate a set of 10, 25, or more to your synagogue or havurah?

A copy of *Real Davvening* can be purchased for $7.95 + $2.50 (shipping & handling) = $10.45. For each additional copy after the first, add: $7.95 + $1.00 (shipping, etc.) = $8.95. See the order form on p. 45. Contact Yitzhak Buxbaum (see p. 48) to inquire about discount rates for 10 or more copies.

☐ Perhaps you might enjoy Volume 2 in The Jewish Spirit Booklet Series:

	An Open Heart:
An Open Heart	The Mystic Path of Loving People
The Mystic Path of Loving People	When Hillel and Rabbi Akiba were asked what the essence of the Torah was, they said: to love your neighbor as yourself. But what is the connection between mysticism and love of neighbor? If one searches in the Kabbalah or in Hasidic Mysticism, love of neighbor does not seem to have the central place that one would expect from the teachings of Hillel and Akiba.
Yitzhak Buxbaum	

An Open Heart explores some traditional sources that reveal the intimate connection between mysticism and loving people and then attempts to more fully integrate religious humanism into the Jewish mystic perspective.

Prices for booklet Volume 2 are the same as for Volume 1 (see above).

☐ Perhaps you might enjoy Yitzhak Buxbaum's books:

Jewish Spiritual Practices

Softcover, 757 pages
List price: $30
Discount price: $25 (+ $3 for shipping, etc.)

"Once in a while I read a book that not only makes a profound impression but radically alters my lifestyle. Such a book is *Jewish Spiritual Practices* . . ." (*Jerusalem Post*).

"*Jewish Spiritual Practices* is a very, very important book, one which the contemporary Jewish world has been in need of for many years. It is . . . the first attempt at a comprehensive guidebook in English to the spiritual dimension of [Jewish religious practices]." (*Wellsprings* [Lubavitch hasidic magazine])

"*Jewish Spiritual Practices* by Yitzhak Buxbaum . . . recently was presented to the Dalai Lama [in India] by an American rabbi who wanted to explain Jewish spirituality to the religious leader." (*Publisher's Weekly*)

The Life and Teachings of Hillel

Hardcover, 376 pages

List price: $35
Discount price: $30 (+ $3 shipping, etc.)

"Buxbaum is a patient and generous religious teacher, writing about Hillel in Hillel's own spirit. This book is filled with learning and profundity, allowing its subject to speak directly to the reader's heart." (Dr. Arthur Green)

Storytelling and Spirituality in Judaism

Softcover, 255 pages

List price: $25
Discount price: $20 (+ $3 shipping, etc.)

The first and only book about sacred storytelling in Judaism and about the hasidic theology of storytelling.

ORDER FORM

To order copies of *Real Davvening, An Open Heart,* or any of Yitzhak Buxbaum's books, send a check payable to Yitzhak Buxbaum, along with this form or a duplicate, to the address on p. 48.

Please send the following:

Title	Quantity	Price (incl. shipping, etc.)
Real Davvening	_____	_____
An Open Heart	_____	_____
Jewish Spiritual Practices	_____	_____
The Life and Teachings of Hillel	_____	_____
Storytelling and Spirituality in Judaism	_____	_____

*NEW YORK STATE RESIDENTS:
For shipments sent to a New York address, add the appropriate sales tax for your area. New York State law requires that tax be paid on the full cost of the order, including shipping.

Subtotal	_____
Sales tax*	_____
TOTAL	_____

You are invited to join
The Jewish Spirit Booklet Club

See the statement about the goals of The Jewish Spirit Booklet Series on p. 2. Club membership only involves receiving information about publication of new booklets. To join, check the box.

☐ Please enroll me in The Jewish Spirit Booklet Club, to be kept informed about forthcoming booklets.

(Print clearly)

_____
Name

_____
Address

_____
City   State   Zip

Maggid
YITZHAK BUXBAUM

Teacher · Storyteller · Author

YITZHAK BUXBAUM is an inspired and inspiring teacher and storyteller, one of those reviving the honorable calling of the *Maggid* (preacher), who in times past travelled from community to community to awaken Jews to the beauty of their tradition.

Mr. Buxbaum teaches and tells stories with warmth and humor. He often sets the mood by leading singing. And he creates the exciting and enlivening atmosphere of a special event, in which everyone is involved.

Judaism is communicated in a way to reach the committed as well as the curious, those who are near, along with those who are now far—but just need someone to offer them a welcome at the door.

Mr. Buxbaum's approach is not denominational or sectarian and is for Jews of all backgrounds. His programs are appropriate for different age-groups: teens, college-age, adults, and seniors.

The programs are entertaining. They are also genuine spiritual experiences. As the Rabbis say: What comes from the heart, enters the heart.

Programs include: LECTURES on topics of Jewish spirituality and mysticism and STORYTELLING of hasidic tales. Inquire about lecture topics.

Mr. Buxbaum leads WORKSHOPS ON DAVVENING that can energize your congregation or havurah. He is available for FULLER SHABBAT PROGRAMS and as a SCHOLAR-IN-RESIDENCE.

Recommendations for
Yitzhak Buxbaum's Teaching and Storytelling

Yitzhak Buxbaum, author of *Jewish Spiritual Practices, The Life and Teachings of Hillel, Storytelling and Spirituality in Judaism,* and *Real Davvening* has lectured and told stories at synagogues, JCC's, Y's, Hillels, and retreats, producing enthusiastic responses. He has taught at CAJE conferences, Havurah Movement Summer Institutes, the Elat Chayyim Jewish Retreat Center, the New York Open Center, the New Age Center (Nyack, N.Y.) and the renowned New School for Social Research (New York, N.Y.).

He was honored by being asked to address an audience of rabbis at The New York Board of Rabbis on the topic "The Quest for Spirituality."

"Many thanks for your presentation and for sharing your wonderful insights and delightful teaching manner with all of us." (Rabbi Jeremiah Wohlberg, President, New York Board of Rabbis)

"Yitzhak Buxbaum is a storyteller in the tradition of the great Hasidic masters. He retells their stories with penetrating insight into their relevance for the great and small actions of our lives. People of all backgrounds are powerfully affected by Yitzhak's unique Jewish presence." (Dr. Herb Levine, Hillel advisor, Franklin and Marshall College, Pa.)

"Yitzhak Buxbaum is a gifted spinner of tales. The audience sits enraptured as he unfolds a tale with skill and warmth." (Rabbi William Berkowitz, former head of the Jewish National Fund and Rabbi of Congregation B'nai Jeshurun, New York, N.Y.)

For a brochure and information about programs, contact:

YITZHAK BUXBAUM, Editor
The Jewish Spirit Booklet Series

144-39 Sanford Ave., Apt. 6D-1
Flushing, New York 11355
(718) 539-5978